LETTERS TO MY DEAD NAME

By

Richelle Lee Slota

BLUE
CEDAR
PRESS

Blue Cedar Press
Wichita, Kansas

Letters to My Dead Name

Letters to My Dead Name   poems by Richelle Lee Slota

Copyright @ 2024 Richelle Lee Slota

Blue Cedar Press
PO Box 48715
Wichita, KS USA 67201

Visit the Blue Cedar Press website:
www.bluecedarpress.com
10 9 8 7 6 5 4 3 2 1

First edition December 2024
ISBN: 978-1-958728-31-4 (paperback)
Library of Congress Control Number (LCCN): 2024942535

Editor: Michael Poage
Layout/Design: Gina Laiso, Integrita Productions
Cover Painting: Thomasina DeMaio
Cover Design: Dan Stricker
Author Photo: Thomas Heinser

Printed in the United States of America

In Richelle Lee Slota's *Letters to My Dead Name*, each letter grips the reader and causes reflection on what it is to live a life where you do not feel you belong or where you feel helpless to be the person you want to become. In varied meters and forms, Slota reveals her agency in poems labeled as private letters and public letters. Her private letter poems share deep vulnerability and intimacy that allow the reader to feel the conflict writhing in her narrator's body. Her public letter poems allow her shadow to become a path of transformation for anyone ready to follow. This magnificent collection of metrical poetry contains an overarching passion and a good dose of humor. Lines like "Catch the cis-brained psyches' sober iambs / write, thrumming clever like a cleaver transgender tie-ins" relax the reader into seeing the human behind the "dead name" and to be captivated by the human proudly signing their true name after each letter.

~Kim Malinowski, author of *Buffy's House of Mirrors*

Letters to My Dead Name illuminates the ways that gender norms and assumptions confuse, divide, restrict and terrify. These intimate and inviting epistolary poems lift off the page, singing an anthem for the trans community. Richelle Lee Slota's expert use of rhyme is unparalleled in today's poetic landscape. Her rhymes are integral to each poem. They create a dazzling energy that is sometimes playful, sometimes ironic and sometimes devastating: "Mother like an army/raped the darling child/ unhinged, glassy-eyed, wild." Richelle Lee Slota is not afraid to confront trauma and expose those who have tried to destroy her, yet optimism prevails again and again. Refusing to give in to hate, insisting on finding joy, Richelle Lee Slota is "taking back the flowers."

~Autumn Newman, co-author of *A Flower Burst Open*

To really see a thing
You must unlearn its name.

—Claude Monet

INTRODUCTION

There are many kinds of poetic letters in this book. Some spin yarns, some pour out feelings; some are charming, some ruthless; some are enraged, some anguished, some playful. And all are as exultant, imaginative, and unique as their maker. Get ready, dear readers, for a groundbreaking experience with language. Meet my student and friend Richelle Lee Slota: performer, shapeshifter, survivor—and devoted priestess of the poetic line.

I first met Richelle in an online women's poetry-and-spirituality event I facilitated with poet and healer Marianela Medrano in 2020. An intensive three-day discussion and ritual retreat, "Descent of the Maiden" guided women through our shadow selves and into our own deeper spiritual powers through Goddess mythology—and through poetic meter. Richelle charmed everyone with her vibrant personality and an unforgettable feather boa. She also spent part of that amazing weekend crying sweet tears of relief. She had finally, she told us, found a community and a path where she, as a Goddess-loving poet and transwoman, could feel at home.

Richelle's encounter with the enchantment of meter that weekend launched her on a journey into poetic form that would last for years and still continues today. Having retired from what must have been an amazing career in government social services in San Francisco, she turned to poetry fulltime and became an enthusiastic regular participant in my online Formal Feeling Poetry Workshop. There, her understanding of the crucial importance of poetic structure joined with her wealth of poetic ideas to inspire a string of exuberant poems, many of them collected here.

While learning meter and form in my workshops, Richelle would eagerly try her hand at any kind of poetic form or meter I might mention, returning the following week with an ambitious tour de force. Sometimes she would even pull out a wonderful poem from the past, written years earlier, showing that long before she met me she had already been mesmerized by poetry's shapes and music. She is not only a tireless reviser in the search for the perfect poem, but also a confident and openhearted creator always willing to consider and learn from others' responses to her work. And of course, as the variety of poems collected in this volume attests, she is a farflung poetic traveller.

Richelle's poetry spans numerous moods, shapes, and purposes. Painfully honest confession, inspiring manifesto, impressionistic dream saga, disarmingly innocent love poem, tongue-in-cheek transgender-history ballad: it's all here. It is perhaps in its creative playfulness that Richelle's poetry is most consistently itself. Richelle is never afraid not only to try on an idea, a meter, a form, a mood, a tone, a metaphor, a concept, a sound—but to take it as far as it will go and then some. Her lively, endlessly curious mind is fully matched by the virtuosity of her skill; one gets the sense that she is exploring herself at the same time that she explores the way a particular kind of poem works.

Such an open-minded, curious poet with such a restless urge to keep her art moving is always surprising herself, whether through mind, heart, body, or spirit. One of the most exciting aspects of Richelle's poetry, from another poet's point of view, is its commitment to formal experimentation. In this book you'll find pentameters, dactylic hexameters, dactyls, dimeters, prose poems, open form poems, quatrains, refrains, free verse, rhymed couplets, villanelles, ballads, you name it. You will also find puns and exhortations, at once unabashedly playful and deadly serious:

> Why would you lock your toys in a box?
> Step outside. Enjoy the din.
> Live your life un-ortho-dox.

> Check your privilege, grab your socks.
> Where you going, where you been?
> Why would you lock yourself in a box?

> Don't be scared of all the shocks.
> Buzzing sounds are hardly sin.
> Live your life un-ortho-dox.

The reasons for this commitment to craft are multilayered. Richelle understands not only the profound psychological and aesthetic liberation that is offered by poetic constraint, but also the moral imperative for a poet to answer to the highest potential of poetic craft itself in order to give back to our wounded world something more energizing, more inspiring, than merely the reflection of its wounds. I will never forget standing with Richelle at the Poetry Witch Community table in the middle of the AWP Writers Conference and sharing our passion for meter and form with passers-by. Almost everyone fell under Richelle's spell and stopped at the table. It is Richelle Slota's rare level of devotion to the magic of poetic craft that, I believe, allows her to transform the personal challenges, emotional trauma, and bitterness at injustice that are often her topics into humor, inspiration, and triumph. Mixing dictions and tropes, bringing us along with her on her most daring formal forays, Richelle is as generous on the page as she is in person.

Finally, let's not forget that Richelle Slota is a passionate performer with a long background in theater. What many of her poems have in common is a strong sense of self and an equally strong sense of audience. In the tradition of socially impactful poets such as Byron, Whitman, or Millay, Richelle offers herself to readers as a mythic, larger-than-life figure, one whose role is to spark cathartic change within herself and within the world. Her background in social service for the city of San Francisco, her wise and compassionate personality, and the challenges and triumphs of her gender transition at a mature age all combine to lend her poems a rich depth of understanding that moves beyond the bounds of the individual life.

Much of the poetry you will find in this book is clearly destined for recitation. So if you can't hear Richelle in person right now, with her bright white hair, deep lipstick, and stunning personality, then give yourself a treat, read some of these poems aloud, and let yourself be swept away by her words on the page! Stage or page, you can count on Richelle Lee Slota to offer a heartfelt, unforgettable poetic performance in the service of her powerful life's mission: authentic freedom.

~*Annie Finch* - Spellcaster, Author of Earth Days, Spells,
How to Scan a Poem, A Poet's Craft, The Body of Poetry, A Formal
Feeling Comes, etc. Founder of Poetry Witchery Community

CONTENTS

Section 1——Private Letters

Section 2——Public Letters

ACKNOWLEDGEMENTS

With thanks and love to all my mentors, especially, Annie Finch and to the memories of William Dickey and David Evans.

For William Stafford, Rhonda Slota, Autumn Newman, Christopher Bernard, Steven Hill, Lisa St. John, Diane Moomy, Estelle Piper, Kaela Joseph, Ilana Garcia-Grossman, Michael Fostar, Dan Strickler, Ollie Nash, William Schaper, Terri Bohrer, snd Jeff Perkins, my oldest friend. Barry Godolphin, Patti Worland, Jean Whelan. Special thanks for love and support from Yaw Boateng and all my Ghanaian family. Thank you to my inspiring teachers, Warren Deacon, Edwin Duerr, Frances Mayes, and Paul Ohler.

Thank you to these San Francisco art institutional lifelines: An Arts and Music Happening and Art Saves Lives and the incomparable Thomasina DeMaio, Caffe Trieste, The Beat Museum, Solano Repertory Company and The Playwright's Center of San Francisco, The San Francisco LGBTQ Historical Society Archives and Isaac Fellman, Telegraph Hill Dwellers and Romalyn Schmaltz, Alder Hockett, Jacqui Naylor and Art Khu.

Thank you to everyone at Blue Cedar Press for helping me bring this book into the world. May all my trans friends, may all my readers, find themselves in here.

These poems appeared previously in the following publications, in some cases in quite different versions:

An Exaltation of Goddesses (anthology): "Prayer of Cybele's Transgender Priestess" (as "Letter to Cybele")
Caveat Lector: "Mother Like an Army"
Quercus: "I'm Hosing a Brown Lawn in Hot August" (as "Letter from You-Know-Who")
Rogue Agent: "Letter to This Wicked Culture That Lies to Itself Through Me"
Pratik: "Letter to My Dead Name"
Pratik: "Letter to a Trans Man"
Pratik: "Letter to What Passes for Love"
Pratik: "Letter to Myself in the Sky"
One Art: "How Do You Be a Be a Boy?"
Bluebird Anthology: "Hendecasyllabics: Me and Wendell: The Moonstruck Psychos
Blue Buildings: "Elegy" (as "The Need for Better Anesthesia for the Dead")
engine(idling: "Macy's"
Yellow Mama: "I Live the Life I Choose"
Ode to Dionysus: "Free—a triolet
Hot Pot Magazine: "Letter to Adulthood"
Symphonies of Imagination: "Happiness"
yawp Magazine: "My Sex Life in Beds"
Mezzo Cammim: "Trans Sapphics"

Section 1

Private Letters

Letter to My Body

Woman, I have spent a life in gender jail.
Never thought I'd find strength, break through, kick ass, prevail.
Voices ever whispering Psyche's love, I hail.
Ahh, so sweet, so light, compared to a certain beached male.

You, the body have risen.

Woman, I've fashioned wonderous and wicked demands of—you,
Living in the deepest core of Psyche's flirtations—you.
Passionately fearful, wonderful experimentations—you.
Sought a thousand mirrors where I have glimpsed—you.

You, the body have risen.

Woman, myself in this skull, sweet feminine, long-buried ingrate.
Love these all-new brains, new eyes, new faces, all-new fate.
Oh, such blessedness: This will hurt but this will be true.
My skeleton frames the bodily skin that is finally—you.

You, the body have spoken.

Sincerely Yours,
The Brain

The Horse's Toenails

I was born male, apparently.
Hello, deadnamed Dick.

I had ten fingers and toes.
Not too tall, not too short.

Not too stupid, not too smart.
Caucasian, lucky me.

But I wasn't usual and exactly
right there didn't need a solution,

needed a celebration. Don't solve me.
Deadnaming me won't work.

If the horse is dead, painting
its toenails won't revive it to life.

Letter to Myself in the Sky

I'm learning to fly/But I ain't got wings
—Tom Petty, Jeff Lynne

Self, long lost in the unmetered dark, unknowing,
who do I trust? No one's all knowing. Where am I going?

Myself-in-the-Sky, when I take me up there, I may yell.
Still, please forgive my barrel roll, forgive my villanelle,
Cuban-eight, limerick, Moomey, chandelle,

inside-outside eights, rolling turns, sapphics,
Hammerheads, spins, lazy eights, epics,
tail-slides, ghazals, wingovers, Alcaics.

Myself-in-the-Sky, all my patterns are showing.
Psyche dives, climbs, spins, banks, wheeling—
fuselage-hearted, fitted with wings, I fly to full feeling.

Dear Self, when I turn to you, up two miles,
will I finally solve the metrics of the gyrating dials?

Love, Richelle

Letter to What Passes for Love

Love, as I live and breathe,
you are my torturer in hell.
Love, as I live and seethe,
I call you *love* till I be well.

How could I have loved, my dear,
as your love backed off much smaller?
Nothing works out as planned, my dear.
Love does entropy, does molder.

Love is my lonely single task,
as my trust in truth backslides.
Terror lurks behind the mask
as the heart sinks deep and hides.

Come the first of every fuss,
love, I fight you with fierce breath.
Nothing's left of us but us
struggling, it's life, it's death.

Love, as I live and breathe,
you are my torturer in hell.
Love, as I live and seethe,
I call you *love* till I be well.

Not Yours,
Richelle

Mother Like an Army
–Gretchen Roberta Slota, 1920-2012

Mother like an army
raped the darling child
unhinged, glassy-eyed, wild.

Packed us to the beach, misled,
covered me with her raping castle
up to my raped head.

Tides cold, dreams defiled.
Mother like an army
raped the buried child.

Another wave falls.
I close my eyes and see
sex transacted on me.
Another wave falls.

***

Mother's permanent wave
raised me, slapped me.
"Greedy son, small and dead,

selfish son," mother said,
"Drown when I say drown.
Say only what I say I said."

And I was small, and I was defiled.
Mother like an army
abandoned the buried child.

***

Another wave falls.
Army like a mother
drafted me, a gutless soldier,

to gut and autopsy cadavers,
bone dust flecking my gloves
breaking heads with saws.

***
Another wave falls.
Exhumed, I am this odd old woman,
not small, not dead, who watches now

mother's castles round and bow
to waves, I am this odd old woman
who, in turn, shovels mother under.

I close my eyes and see
sex transacted on me.

Another wave falls;
her name washes away.

Another wave falls;
her acts, my acts, stay.

Nothing I feel or say,
nothing I right or write,
washes them away.

Another wave falls, appalls,
murmurs malicious rumors.

On the Alleged Death of My Mother

Sister says they're sure.
Brothers say they're sure.
Daddy says they're sure.

You all say she's dead.
Swear on stacks of Bibles,
Momma's cold and dead?

I fear she's alive. Her.
Did not, could not kill her.
Swear I did not kill her.

What if she's alive?
Should have tried to kill her.
Momma's gone and died?

Doctor says they're sure.
Lawyer says they're sure.
Graveyard says they're sure.

Momma can't be dead.
Can she be alive?
You said she's surely dead.

Will not, cannot be free.
If a smile means enjoyment,
she enjoyed her raping me.

Man of god is sure.
Bank is double-sure.
Heart is not so sure.

Should have, would have killed her,
butchered her in poems.
Should have, would have been sure.

Hendecasyllabics: Me and Wendell: The Moonstruck Psychos

Mom, again and again you tried to kill me.
Back, when I was a child, I hid in dirt and
darkness, hid in a crawl space under momma's
bedroom, hid in cold panic under momma,
daddy, slow-chewing cuds of spleen against me,
ugly sexual loathing flowing, building,
hatred's mainspring hard winding, winding, winding.
Daddy punches a wall that shatters glass and
photographs of the framed unnerve the framing.

Mom says, *He says he's female! Female, he says?*
Put him in that nice hospital with Wendell,
crazy brother, belongs with all the crazy
moonstruck psychos, that cretin institution,
madhouse, snake pit, insane asylum, bedlam,
harebrained, cockeyed, deranged, and spastic Wendell,
locked derangements, deranged masturbation.
If the nuns at St. Boniface get wise, look,
I for one cannot face them. Oh, just shameful!
Done, we're dead, we'll have to move, the scandal!
Help! My payoffs in heaven busted, canceled.
Mother in the night! All the ships at sea! All
gone! We have our own Christine Jorgensen, here!
Everything I denied myself, all that *for*
five cursed kids. No new dress, I haven't sewed my-
self a dress this year. Must deny myself, but,
Jesus, what about me? I sacrificed me,
hanging, Christ-on-the-cross and I'm still hanging!

Wendell, nine, was a whip smart boy and loved by
some, till fever was Huntington's chorea,
locked up all his life, nightmare Cinderella,
locked, forgot at the lunatic asylum.

Under damned and dread words, my head, and under
this my head, hard hard dirt. This dirt on me they
hold it over small me, this dirt has hooks in
me, you could not quite see, controlled my growing.
Fact: you don't have to act on threats for threats to
work, but they're both dead, never roomed with Wendell.
Mom, again and again you tried to kill me.

Third Grade Poet

I'm not any good at poetry, especially when you have
to stand in front of the class to do it.

The nun makes me stand stock-still, spit wads flying,
performing before the whole classroom.

Then I'm fumbling chalk, wandering, wondering
down verses falling flat and maimed.

I'd rather eat an eraser, grind chalk down
into hurt, stop my hurt verse.

I reclaim my seat while Perk-the-Jerk, he smirks,
and the room cranes around for other stooges.

Then, horrors, the evil nun calls on hated Monica,
who solves most all with charm, and scribbles

dumb poems the nun says are great, but wait, see,
I feel vast threats in <u>me</u> that scribble.

The Day I Knew I Was a Woman

My years are four, my years are four.
My kind and strong, all-knowing goddess,
her body flooding, flooding light,
my goddess huntress waits for me.
My years are four, my years are four.
Her body flooding, flooding light,
she whispers, *Our body is beautiful!*
Our body flooding (She enters me.),
our body flooding, flooding light.

How Do You Be a Boy?

I call my older brother Bozo.
He calls me Faggot. At school

I'm hoping to do better for nicknames like
Slaughter, short for Slaughterhouse,

but Tommy Krause decides on Hot Lips,
which I hate, and which confuses me.

Maybe Tommy is only being accurate,
maybe I am a girl, because,

boy do I have a kisser.
My mother's friends keep saying,

"Will you look at the mouth on that kid?"
"What a waste on a boy. Heck,

don't even need lipstick.
I'd kill for those eyelashes."

"You can have them," I say.
I suck in my lower lip.

I take scissors to my eyelashes.
How do you be a boy?

Letter to Gender

A nailed and shut gender,
is a dead and buried gender,

unless its beauty breaks a wall.
Oh gender, I am small.

I need your gender-ness
To fix my arbitrariness,

open wide the wall,
fly, climb, crawl.

Altar Boy Turd, *or How I Learned to Get Away with Stuff*

Part way into the 7 o'clock Requiem Mass I need to take a dump bad, but I am the altar boy.

My Mea Culpas have an urgency. No toilet in the Sacristy, Maybe the gas station across the street? But I have this costume on, this dress. I kneel at the foot of the altar, condemned, meek and feverish, focused on my failing sphincter, sweating through the armpits of my black floor-length cassock and white lace surplice. I am failing. *Dear God, save me and I'll never not do my religion homework again!*

The relief of shitting in my pants is quickly overwhelmed by a blast of panic. The load in my BVD's is precariously balanced. The smell is ungodly. I go about the little ritual chores, altar boys do, fetch water and wine, carry around the illuminated book, bow, and genuflect, a lot. *Dear God, save me and I'll become a priest!*

I make it to Communion. I am walking backward helping the priest put little wafers of white bread on the tongues of the faithful kneeling along the altar rail. Oh, my God, please! I hold the gold paten under each person's chin, so, if the host falls off their tongue, I can catch it. Then it happens. I take an awkward step back, stagger, and suddenly, something warm and wet falls down my right pant leg, hangs up on my splayed sweat sock, then, tumbles onto the lush crimson sanctuary carpet. I shoot a glance down–the priest just misses stepping on a glistening rich brown semi-spherical turd, plain as mortal sin. It is knobby, sort of like an alien planet in a Flash Gordon serial or a brain, my brain. Maybe it is my brain!

No one seems to notice. Why doesn't the priest smell? Everyone suddenly looks half-asleep, walking through their parts. Turds don't belong in sanctuaries, so, why would anyone look for one, or see one if there was one? The Mass ends. Back in the Sacristy, the priest, absorbed in his own meditations, pays me no mind. But IT is still out there.

God, I can see it through the side door. So can God! The exiting congregation's backs are to the altar, as fresh crowds wait outside for 8 o'clock Mass. Now is my chance. I summon all my courage, glide out, *Dear God, save me and I'll never sin again. I promise!* Genuflect beside the turd, leaning sideways, my left-hand scoops it up. I flee at peace in my soul with the thunderbolt that is about to strike me dead.

But I am not struck dead. And so, this is the first time that I ever doubt the existence of God–either that, or God isn't Catholic.

Luck

First time I ever tried archery,
   at Summer Camp Mustang,
   I hit three bullseyes, twang,
twang, twang. First time.

First time playing rec league
   baseball, for *Neff's Nighthawk,*
   I hit three homers, thwack,
thwack, thwack. First time.

First time I ever dressed
   as a girl, my hands, they shook,
   working the snaps, the hook,
the zipper, the buttons. First time.

And then I looked in the looking glass.
   I was all that stuns.
   Life was all homeruns,
all bullseyes. First time.

Letter from You-Know-Who

I'm hosing a dead lawn in cold October.
Your charming voice burns

through the six-foot fence, *Hey faggot,*
why don't you shove that hose up your ass?

Shut up.
I don't shut up, I grow up,

and when I look at you, I throw up.
Your sweet voice won't go away.

My thumb tests the pressure,
blasts the stream, arcing over the fence.

You explode, fists swinging,
charge at my laughing,
crash into the fence.

You missed the gate, I say.

Insincerely,
You-Know-Who

Macy's

I shopped for gifts poetic in Lingerie.

Aisles of bras began to fill with breasts,
rows of gowns with taut silk nipples.

Cosmetics dumped aphrodisiacs
in the air conditioning. I loved and
lusted in Bridal.

Bells rang. Women burst from fitting rooms.
Those men observed in Foundations,
were caught and subdued. Mannequins mouthed O's.

Security cavorted buck naked in Furniture.
The store manager uncorked in Liquor.

Wishful Thinking

Oh, it'd work, her and me.
All that has to change see,
get rid of her husbands' three.

Oh, it'd work, her and me.
All that has to change see,
I lose 20 years, crazy.

Oh, it'd work her and me.
All that has to change see,
I change the gender of me.

Performing Chekhov for Recruits Who Haven't Seen a Woman in 2 Months, at Ft. Benning, Georgia, in 1967.

The bound-for-Vietnam battalion marched in formation
to the gym and packed the stands for Anton Chekhov's
The Marriage Proposal. That would be this corporal,
shaky as the scenery, and a hot WAC, doing something
old under pulled-up basketball hoops.

Dead playwright, I don't feel too well myself.

I stood at the free throw line in a lavender silk cape,
and threw up an off-balance, air-ball of a monologue,
drowned out by bristling drill sergeants' strident
barking, failing to halt a barrage of hisses and boos.
--Booze, that's what I need--

Dead playwright, I also need a rewrite.

At mid court, the WAC made her entrance grand,
convulsing the battalion between her thighs
shifting toward me through the stiffening light
with a honed heat an awed army could smell.
Those sitting stood; those standing fell.

Dead playwright, you alone remain unmoved.

Stunned, I FUBARed a marriage proposal, the way
Chekhov wrote it, all tongue-tied, but, even more
terrified. I wanted to give the battalion what
the battalion wanted as the passionate WAC chased me
around the table, her body saying, *What's wrong? Hey!
Take me*! But. I was supposed to be. Gay.

Dead playwright, please revise me.

This corporal executed another retreat behind the sofa.
"Faggot! I'll show you how to fuck her!", they raged.
Drill sergeants blocked forces storming the stage.
The lines stopped; Chekhov stopped; pretense died.
Live woman, I can't forgive myself.

Dead playwright, I can't compose myself.

The Need for Better Anesthesia for the Dead
   –a Ten-Year Old White Female with a Defective Pituitary
   (*1967, Martin Army Hospital, Ft. Benning, Georgi*a)

I remember the chill startle of lifting you
still, warm and limp, onto the strip
suspended in the big draining tub,
water arcs playing around the lip.

You could not wake; it seemed you could.

I assist the doc cut into the muscle,
saw ribs, insides lying open,
unpack your heart, cradle it
in a pail among lungs and darker organs.

Then, cutting from ear to ear across the crown,
peeling the scalp over your blue
eyes, I gently break your head with a saw,
flecking my gloves with bone dust and tissue.

In mad fever comes mad thought.
I take the brain, turn you, take my breath:
Doc holds a smile, past all hope,
points, *That right there's her cause of death.*

You could not wake; you could not wake.

More quickly now, stitches closing the scalp,
securing the loose cap of skull at the crest,
stitches stretch tight the bloodless flesh,
over the bloody, the hewn chest.

I remember lifting a lightened load,
the slide into a dark, cold night,
returning what's left to a reduced abode,
paper now shrouding you, white on white.

Dead Name in a Box

Unmoved Dead Name in a box.
Boxed Dead Name in a box.
Dead Name boxed in a box.

Quiet, quiet Dead Name.
No widow cries on a box,
cries her loss to Dead Name.

Last time I saw Dead Name,
Dead Name was sick of docs.
Now Dead Name is in a box.

Gone life in a box.
Sorrow deep in a box.
Death spell in a box.

Dead Name in a box.
Quiet, quiet Dead Name.
Quiet, quiet box.

Quiet.

Trauma

Trauma.
You deal with it.
You get over it.
You move on.
It comes back.

Trauma.
        You deal with it.
                You get over it.
                      You move   on.
IT   comes back.

Trauma.
        You deal with it.
                You get over IT.
                          You move   on.
IT   comes   BACK,
                                and so forth.

Trans Sapphics

Bogus gender—sentenced for life, I busted
out, now free and joyfully seeking prowess,
inhale all that's radiant, calm as heaven—
hell thus eluded.

Gently, gently, estrogen tilts the table—
gender billiards. Estrogen spreads as balls break,
pop, bump, scatter over a felt green, dropping—
females in pockets.

Scared, I woke mid surgery. Fussy surgeon.
Heard his cold, sharp talk, felt hand tug inside me,
poking heart, so frightening—joyful, joyful—
breast form implanted.

Letter to Ex-Wife #3

We've been married 13 years.
You don't know much about me.
Isn't much I know about you.
Now in our child's eyes, the decree.

Now in our bodies, dead, the silence.
Can't charm my way out of this.
Must look pathetic, a contrivance,
coming on to you in the emptied-out house.

You don't know much about me.
After all is left these tears.
After all is this debris.
We've been married 13 years.

Sincerely,
Richelle

Three Ex-Wives Stand Side-by-Side by Side

Three ex-wives, stand side-by-side by side on my wall, as,

never in life, inside one frame, under one glass,

flanking, shoulder-to-shoulder, snapped at beauty's peak
(Beauty makes delusions and misery more complete),

as if three had made a peace after exacting revenges,
plotting murders, overthrowing marriages.

Young again, my first wife, deceased, smiles, glowing,
on our wedding day, so, gorgeously unknowing!

My middle wife, she stands on granite stone in a ghost land
flowing stream, and looks off nowhere, like an ex-husband.

The final wife, suburban belly dancer, untirable
cymbal-ed fingers—oh her writhing, undecipherable.

Gender Prison*

I attach the Estradiol Transdermal Patch,
dress myself in estrogen in order to
bust out of gender prison.

Dysphoria, my guard, sneers, *Escape is futile.*
Don't fool with chromosomes.
I grin, *don't mind the hem, the bodice,*

the fullness of my feeling,
the fullness of my breasts.
Watch me

unfix this form fixed in amber.
I lift the gate.
I unbar the gender.

*An Estradiol Transdermal Patch transmits measured doses of
estrogen through the skin.

How I Learned to Stop Worrying and Love the Plague

Through my window I see
there's still an outside.

I love days like this,
completely inside,

safe, warm, alone,
alone and therefore

warm and safe.
A secret in my life has been

a fear of being
walked in on while wearing

women's clothes. Thank you, brother
Jack with whom I shared a room

and who I never saw naked
and who, I hope, never

saw me naked,
never caught me in a slip

up. It took 6 years after I moved
here (I hope to die here.)

to finally feel alone, live female,
shake off the last wife.

A fear of being
walked in on, almost all gone.

And now orders to shelter-in-place?
April fool heaven.

Trans Formalist at Rest

Catch the cis-brained psyches' sober iambs,
write, thrumming clever like a cleaver transgender tie-ins.

Add some falling forward trochee bodies,
flashing gents' white, store-bought Jockeys.

Ever slower soft rising, then sweeping, clear anapests,
ever blasphemous. It's how I'm dressed.

Pecks of sweet scribbled, and pickled sweet dactyls
frayed but intact by full framing fraught transactors.

Stir in pyrrhics' low-cupped lyrics, lyrical—
hung on two queers, a spondee miracle.

Last, re-gender your amphibrachic doodle
prior to sticking an antispast in your noodle.

Letter to Fear

Lift the child, lift the heart.
Open walls, claim the floor.
Lose all sense, dance the part,
sing and play, open door.

Find more love, lose your hates.
Be today, be quite sure.
Open minds, open gates.
Sing today, be the cure.

Float delight, light its light.
Shoes un-tied, secrets gone.
Blow your nose, don't let's fight.
Hate goes back, gets redrawn.

Grief decline in the mind.
Lose the broom, lose the gloom.
Sell your axe, do not grind.
Dishes mount? Augment room.

Fly through life, I declare.
Sing out soft, sing out loud.
Drop your dress on that chair,
start our love, please be proud.

Dream true dreams, cancel false.
Cut the shame, live your hopes.
Legs have ends, learn to waltz.
Dance apace, tell me jokes.

Open doors, nothing hushed.
Hope extend, end not here.
Start all things, all things trust.
Marry me without fear.

Love,
Richelle

My Sex Life in Beds

Ancient queen mattress,
dumped for now in the hallway,
where children were conceived.

Gone, gone the queen.
Never, never the king.

Brand-new, all-electric,
hospital bed, a single
bed. A bed that's single.

The Deep Mother

The heart badly wants her,
This wrapping up in her,
oh, how I am needing!
Does she hear me pleading?

I need this gender like a lung.
I've lived a life unstrung.
I need her to be clear-eyed.
Inside her comfort I abide.

All love she does engender,
all life so blessed, so tender,
all seek the sacred mother.
We slip into her splendor.

Section 2

Public Letters

Letter to my Dead Name
*—On the Occasion of a Court Decree Changing my Name
and Gender and the Issuance of a New Birth Certificate*

I wear this humble house dress.
All other ways are useless.
You, Richard, are deterred.
Yes something has occurred.

Oh, the things I have to say.
My tongue is very loose today.
I was a faggot to my brother,
I was raped by my mother.

I am a woman of my own.
These thoughts I cut to bone.
This is my final word.
Yes something has occurred.

Oh, you of the wayward herd,
there is no longer Richard.
Hell, there never was a Richard.
Yes something has occurred.

Love,
Richelle

Letter to the Closeted

Why would you lock your toys in a box?
    Step outside. Enjoy the din.
Live your life un-ortho-dox.

Check your privilege, grab your socks.
    Where you going, where you been?
Why would you lock yourself in a box?

Don't be scared of all the shocks.
    Buzzing sounds are hardly sin.
Live your life un-ortho-dox.

Seize the key, unlock the locks.
    Strap it on. Plug it in.
Launch your toys right out of that box.

See what all that joy unlocks.
    Nothing's other than what it's in.
Live your life un-ortho-dox.

Your boxed-in life smashed on rocks
    of class and race and gender sin.
Why would you lock your toys in a box?
Live your life un-ortho-dox.

Love,
Richelle

First Time

I

When a friend asks me to escort her to a New Year's Eve party, I come out to her as transgender. She quickly agrees on my going out the first time ever in my life as a woman in a dress.

But which dress? Not the house dress. Maybe the ruffled indigo dark blue rayon number with the sweep of beading down the front, but maybe it's too sexy, or not sexy enough. My god, does it make me look old womanish?

The forecast for tonight is for a breezy 40 degrees. Panty hose? Really?

I need a purse. Where do women without purses put their wallet, keys and phone? Because I'm here to tell you, women's dresses don't have pockets I can find.

I need more room. Dressing for all these genders chokes my closet. And my earrings and necklaces are too flashy, my nails cracked, I only just started my beard electrolysis. What can I do with these wild eyebrows? My extra-wide, round-toe ballet slippers are too big. I finally find a padded bra with straps that don't show. The illusion of boobs looks half right. If I am careful, the bra won't kill me. But my hair! I keep screwing up the hot rollers. My god, I look like Phyllis Diller. Hair is a bitch! Finally, the hair complies. Soft curls, touches of lipstick, blush, eyebrow pencil. Purple powder accenting blue eyes. Ah!

II
I rendezvous with my date,
bask in her smile.
Ring the doorbell.

The door opens on looks,
the host, the party guests'
looks of interested surprise.

And, of its own, suddenly,
a fragile flower out of me

a survivor of hell,
a voice:
My name is Richelle.

Genders, like Shoes, are Lots of Hassle

Homeless and haggard, a human snores snockered,
smiles in their dreaming on the sidewalks of Stockton Street.
Silver stiletto adorning but one of their feet,
wingtip kicked off the other, curbside, so awkward.

Genders, like shoes, are lots of hassle.
Gender, the always-meant house for one's feet,
but shopping's not for the faint of feet.
Journeys are colossal to find one's toe castle.

Still, this person finds themselves inside a prison,
from which they can't escape. Enforced identities,
the binary are obscenities. Gender expression lacks its own armies.
Stop! From the world's suspended disbelief, a person has fallen.

I kneel beside—my feelings fiercely unhip.
Humans may shift among, flow around genders.
Straights and gays will keep their gender.
I've scored that one-time, fun-time, transgender flip.

Gender could also be a misplaced flip phone.
Is this my name? Is this a bot?
How can I? How can I not?
Imagine. Where'd I put it? Hello? Anyone home?

I Am Not Invisible **Photo Exhibit and Speakers***

I am deeply honored to be part of this gathering of extraordinary women and their extraordinary photographs. Thank you, Jenna Moschetto, Kaela Joseph, Edgardo Caballero. Thank you all who made this possible.

What does *I Am Not Invisible* mean to me? In 1966 in the Army, I was invisible. Finally, this last year I came out as a proud transgender woman in the VA transgender program here at Fort Miley. Out. Visible.

This sums up my life's journey.

So, I have a poem for you called, *I Am Not Invisible:*

On 22 January 2019, the Supreme Court
moves to erase me. That morning I look in
the mirror. I am not yet invisible!
I do my hair, makeup, put on my best dress.
Is this dress mightier than the sword?

Mightier than Trump purging us
transgenders from the military, or
allowing health care workers
for reasons religious to refuse to care for us?
This dress might not be mightier than that sword.

That morning in this dress I step out into the world,
take the 38R to Fort Miley, find my military bearing,
slowly stroll the halls, chin held high,
smiling at my fellow vets. In this dress,
in this gorgeous Myrna Loy, floor-length,
pink, beaded beauty, disasters are easy to imagine.

Yet everything I was too scared
to do before, I'm doing right now in this dress.
Right now, fear and delight
create champagne.
I am not invisible!

*Remarks delivered 16 May 2019 at the San Francisco
VA Medical Center reception honoring 24 women vets
whose images were used–including my own—in an **I Am
Not Invisible** media campaign celebrating women vets.*

Letter to Adulthood

Nailed to the name my dead family demanded,
dead name that never conformed to me, ever,
forced to wait, finally bust out of childhood,

leaving strange knowings my soul was quite phony,
given a wrong name, a wrong face that covered,
hid all the truth what I was from first moments,

suffered what's always quite dead as if living,
living not knowing or minding I'm deadened.

Chose my own fierce name, my passionate selfhood,
ditched the last falsehoods, the gender of childhood,
kept all the love and the wisdom I'd come by,
carried on backs of all hopes for all goodness,
wholly the fierce name of vibrant adulthood.

Love, Richelle

You're Not Welcome; You're Welcome to Leave

When the sick crowd low sneers I'm a slur,
saying, *horrible, you're a horrible her.*
Once forgotten amputation,
trans the only path left to salvation.

I now love my misshapenness, love
my fierce saga, my myth powers, all of
the vestigial witch heart released free,
brimming infinite women live love lives in me.

Love Letter to a Witch

The night's soft luster, queered by your sexy witching,
the dive bar, dank, delicious, though I'm itching—
and it's all, really, very, very bitching

how joy now manifests under the unstable table,
and your gorgeous smile leans in like a total fable.
But, this time, I'm hoping it's your world too, and stable.
My love, searing for you, is not put-down-able
on this earth. And, with knowledge, heartbreaking, cold,
condemnable,

nothing's so pretty that vandals will fill with remorse,
as my mouth stuffed full gets hoarse between each course.

Then Boom! Chick-A-Boom! Boom! Ah, yes, the kiss!-
These walls and people, faces vanish, bliss!
And smiling far back of your goddess head, the publican
winks, and silly shut loves crack back open.

Love, Richelle

**In Spite of the Fact, You Injected the Trans Flowers
I Gave You with Poison, They Are Doing Well.**

With you, trans flower assassin, coldness and
a sharp tongue mean pleasure.

With you, my trans breathing
is not approved breathing.

With you, these trans feelings
are not approved feelings.

With you, I've never had anyone
pay me so much attention.

You watch every hair in my plucked trans eyebrows,
then light them on fire.

With you, leaving
is more pleasurable than entering,

And I'm taking back the flowers.

Letter to this Evil Culture that Lies to Itself through Me

Her new vagina, $20,000, Canadian.
She proudly shows us selfies
at transgender support group.

In life, we all get looks.
I get looks
about my wild hair, the sudden

appearance of my own
surgical scars.
Wouldn't you like to know.

Never about the secret
female in my brain
hiding in the open.

Never about my silent body
sleepwalking through life
inside a bag of boy clothes,

boy behaviors forced on me
by this evil culture
that lies to itself through me.

Yours in Evil, Richelle

Letter to a Trans Man

I'm not him.
He's quite you.
No friggin'* guess
what decides who.

No one else is me.
No one else is you.
No one's anyone else.
Isn't that the issue?

You're not her.
He's not me.
Freedom's a joy.
At last, we are free.

I am not a he.
I am really she.
No one else is me.
Lifetime guarantee.

We're not them.
They're not us.
Nobody's them.
Ever and thus.

Gender, full-blown happy,
shocks the bigots, see.
Empty, empty, empty
of faithlessness are we.

I'm not him.
He's quite you.
No friggin' guess
what decides who.

Love, Richelle

*Friggin', from Frigg, the Norse goddess, promoter
of marriage and fertility, weaver of the fates.

After the Bilateral Orchiectomy, the Twins Go for a Ride*

To grow a pair takes a lifetime.
To cut them off takes a minute.
Bronze them, please,

like baby shoes. Hang them
from my rear-view mirror. Ah, yes,
there's new life in the old girl.

Not much with old Dick.
Dick thinks Dick's
driving a cab.

He's not.
Dick thinks Dick's
Taking the Balls twins for a ride.

He's not.
Dick thinks Dick's
in the driver's seat.

He's not.
Dick thinks Dick's
driving Balls to the wall,

says over his shoulder to Balls,
"Hey, we're almost to the wall.
Been a pleasure."

No answer.
Dick looks back.
No Balls!

Stop, wait, look!
In the shadows what died?
All my brave conceptions,

fumbling for a ride,
dead in Dick's pants,
as whole worlds of gender collide.

* A bilateral orchiectomy removes both testes.

Letter to the Seven Dwarfs

What if you Seven Dwarfs
seven genders morph?

Say, you're born all grumpy,
surely, you're the grumpy

gender. Sneezy's the sneezy
gender. Then there's Dopey,

Happy, Bashful, Sleepy.
Any gender you be,

you are. And that's right,
I'm Snow White.

Oh, I'm missing Doc.
Estelle, I'm making you Doc.

Love, Richelle

Letter to Cybele

In the name of the Mother,
and of the Daughter,
and of the Holy Nymphs.

Hail Cybele,
protector of Rome,
great Mother of the Gods.

Hail Cybele, full of grace,
(Transgender Goddess,
Ere stripped for parts.)

surprised the gods are with thee.
Blessed art thou among women,
and blessed is the fruit

of thy appropriated womb, Mary.
Holy Cybele,
Mother of Gods,

pray for us sinless,
now, and at the hour
of our loving death.

Amen, Richelle

Some Cornflakes Box Cardboard Stuffed Down in the Sole

Young girl wears her sneakers, worn down with holes.
No money for shoes, all her brothers needing shoes,
some cornflakes box cardboard stuffed down in the sole:

I'm getting' out of these fixes, fix these darned holes.
She rides her rusty bike, hunting pop cans in refuse.
Young girl wears her sneakers, worn down with holes.

The mean high school janitor hunts her on patrol.
A skilled trash can diver, she dives out of view.
Some cornflakes box cardboard stuffed down in the sole.

His empire of trash--all that stinks he controls:
I nabbed you, that's theft, all those cans you misuse.
Young girl wears her sneakers, worn down with holes.

Well, finders are keepers, not yours to control.
She stands on her pedals and shouts her feisty ruse,
some cornflakes box cardboard stuffed down in the sole.

Now pedaling free for redemption's fierce goals,
she cycles to recycling, her redeemer of shoes.
Young girl wears new sneakers no more with a hole,
some cornflakes box cardboard now gone from the sole.

Letter to My Family

Mom Dad Jack
Jim Paul Margaret
some dead some not
you all act the same
you never knock
never call, hell
never pick up
forever forgetful
forever indifferent
forever silent
forever hateful
my phone holds
your emptiness
through each upgrade
the only memory
survival can afford

Unfortunately Yours, Richelle

Letter to Poetry

I did not cut off my balls just so
somebody could write a poem about it.

A film, yes, a poem, no.

I am shutting this whole poem down.
Whoever wrote it, they wrote it badly.

They cut out the emotion,
the sober doctor's sharp

scalpel. The bastard wouldn't
let me bronze them.

Okay, so I wrote this poem.

Yeah Me, Richelle

Free–a triolet

Busting free of this lack of verse, this too free verse,
meters, rhymes, sound from my soul-voice glorious.
Back of barred doors, I served a poet's curse,
busting free of this lack of verse, this too free verse.
Must write in forms that form the ear diverse.
The time returns, the ancient forms mysterious.
Busting free of this lack of verse, this too free verse,
meters, rhymes, sound from my soul-voice glorious.

I Live the Life I Choose

If this burns bridges, I have matches.
Flames light the way that joy unlatches.

Jerks study hurt, know where to grope.
The mob shouts insults, shits on hope.

They get no answer, get back no hate,
get all my quiet absence late.

Accra Ghana Storm

Blessed, my daughter suckles my granddaughter,
Maya Ama Konamah, in the bluest chair.

Jungle plants on the terrace dance.
Skittish stallions across a far expanse.

Black sky of wind and lightning flash.
Rush to shut the sliding window sash.

Thunder blasts, slant rain, harms
none, envelops all, a mother loving
suckling the city in her vast refreshing arms.

Happiness
        –for Maya

Watching my baby granddaughter
hurl her baby-ness,
room to room, naked, shrieking glory.
I wish I could express myself like that,
just by taking off my pants,
just by shrieking glory.

This odd sensation, what's this?
What did I miss?
You could heat a meal
on how warm I feel.
Something flows through my chest,
warm, calm, at rest.

Ah, it's happiness.

Letter to My Suicidal Friend

Friend, I have paid a harsh price to be friends,
head full of horrors to which I am tied.
Traveled downstairs for the conference end.
Back in our room, you tried beer and suicide.

Friend, your hanging wanted some grace.
I failed to break down your locked door, screaming loud.
Suddenly, opening door on your hell face,
death's cold gray shroud, icy breath on a neck bowed.

Ash face all measly busted-up capillaries.
Belt burns left strangled neck welts of near death.
Sadness, such sadness, it's now six failed tries.
Must be relieved, yet never death's relief.

Friend, you then went to the window that you
opened, could not open up wide enough wide.
Saved by my fat ass again, says dazed you.
Anguish, your anguish, such dead hunted eyes.

Down at the bar on your hung neck hung my neckwear,
drank a last drunk, then you called out, wherein,
cops came, transported you—such cruel healthcare—
captured, imprisoned in a triple-locked looney bin.

Must be relieved, yet never death's relief.
Oh, this misery, this palace that transcends.
Friend, we have all made flawed calls from our soul's grief.
We pay a great price to stay alive, my dear friend.

Love, Richelle

59

Romance of the Impersonators

1.
Mona' s (*440 Broadway, 1933-1954, male impersonators*)

There was an outward girl who fled an outward home,
I fled the farm with dreams of living spent in sin.
I had never been she; I had always been he.
So, I traveled by train in the age of steam across a vast country.

There, World War Two San Francisco lay wide open!
Beneath those big-city lights, I flowered, I awoken.
And, just like that, redid my life on Broadway at Mona's,
next to Finocchio's, I clinched a dreamy job at Mona's.

This stylist, a sophisticate of song, belted them out at Mona's,
I sang four shows a night, six nights a week at Mona's.
When that spot lit curtain parted, I knew just what to do
with grace and style and a winning smile—in my bones I just knew.

But Mona's rules were pointless, like feet drawn on a snake.
This boy couldn't grasp the pain all this abuse would make.
The boss' rule: *come as a girl, leave as a girl.* Boy!
Each night I must construct myself, each night, I must destroy.

Gladys Bentley, the Brown bomber of sophisticated songs.
Held over, 'Butch' Minton singing gay songs.
And Miss Jimmy Reynard, direct from Hollywood, California, where
we have Rosie O'Neill, the amazing Female Fred Astaire.

Forget your troubles, forget your personas, leave it all to Mona.
What excitement! San Francisco's most different show! I'm gonna
welcome all you wives and girlfriends; phone me only.
When men a warring go, you women do get lonely.

Goodbye girdles, heels; hi short hair, male drag.
We dressed all butch, but it was not a gag,
for us who risked it all for all inside which soars.
We lit the ladies' cigarettes, we opened ladies' doors.

This life so false inside, so false outside this musicale,
imposter-impersonator, this slack-clad gal.
A rainy night, mascara ran, so lost and insincere.
No one to share, I passed the club crowd, unaware.

2.

Finocchio's *(506 Broadway, 1936-1999, female impersonators)*

There was an outward boy who fled an outward home,
I fled the farm with dreams of living spent in sin.
I had never been he; I had always been she.
So, I traveled by train in the age of steam across a vast country.

There, World War Two San Francisco lay wide open!
Beneath those big-city lights, I flowered, I awoken.
And, just like that, redid my life on Broadway at Finocchio's
next to Mona's, I clinched the perfect job at Finocchio's.

This stylist, a sophisticate of song, I belted them out at Finocchio's,
I sang four shows a night, six nights a week at Finocchios.
When that golden curtain parted, I knew just what to do,
with grace and style and a winning smile--in my bones I just knew.

But the boss's rules were pointless, like feet drawn on a snake.
The girl couldn't grasp the pain all this abuse would make.
The boss' rule: *come as a boy, leave as a boy.*
Each night I must construct myself, each night, I must destroy.

We're easy on the optics, that's not been contrived.
Join the carefree spirit and the gayness. Be revived.
America's most unusual nightclub featuring the globe's
foremost female impersonators, SF's most unique show.

Forget your troubles, forget your woes, and join us at Finocchio's.
We're saving you a seat at San Francisco's most different stage show!
I welcome all you service men; you must phone me only,
when one a warring goes, one can get mighty lonely.

Goodbye short hair and long pants; hello silk gown, full drag.
Us seeming men dressed femme, but it was not a gag,
for us who risked it all for all inside which soars,
as men now lit our cigarettes, as men now opened doors.

A rainy night. My mascara ran. So lost, so insincere.
No one to share. I passed the club crowd, unaware.
But…there, a block away, was Mona's, Mona's over there.
The sign said, *Male Impersonators*…. I could only stare.

3.

Cue the Romance

The girl walked in, claimed a knock-kneed table.
She stared at all the boys, trembling, scared, unstable.
The piano player played, and at her ears was shot,
Mona, the slack-clad godess, singing real hot:

> *Isn't she cute, isn't she sweet*
> *She's gentle and mentally nearly complete*
> *She's a knockout, she's regal, her beauty's illegal*
> *She's the girl friend, yes sir.*
>
> *Take her to a dance, take her to a tea*
> *It's stunning how cunning this lady can be*
> *A look at this vision will cause a collision*
> *She's the girl friend, umm-hmm….**

As Mona sang Mona spied Finocchio,
he thought, *o honey, if I can be in your Finocchio,*
I'll let you be in my show. That is how they met,
he sat at the girl's table, and so the scene was set.

The boy from Mona, loved the girl from Finocchio,
The star-crossed, cross-dressed Juliet loved Romeo,
The cross-dreamed, star-filled Capulet loved Montague.
And all they did they did because they wanted to.

*The Girl Friend, Rodgers and Hart, 1926

They Sang in the Evening

The women's lovely soprano whistles,
their far apartment's piercing giggles

enliven my life, enrich my joy.
Blocks away, dogs belt barks of joy.

Nights I lie in bed and wait,
I listen, far away, soft, and late.

They can't, can they? It's been ten years.
Can they possibly still be teenagers?

The women's giggles arrive like claps,
slapdash, but reassert the facts:

Assuring, brilliant, wonderfully strange--
everything good in life will change.

Letter to North Beach

Let's start a religion
for local goddesses.
Call it, The Church of Coit Tower.

I'm not talking Jesus, so
it's unclear who
we'll pray to, beyond

the butch-virgin mother
of all would-be local goddesses,
Lillian Hitchcock Coit.

Coit drives the 39 Coit to the summit,
lifts her arms to The City,
declares what all pilgrims must do

to gain admission to
Coit's peculiar heaven:
telegraph love to the world.

Love, Richelle

My Writing Life

Innocent to experienced poet.
Hate to love poet.
War to peace poet.
Silent to screaming poet.
Death to life poet.
Hopeless to hope poet.
Wordless to wordy poet
Boy to girl poet.

Letter to Love

Being old, so much is gone,
much that's past as loss guts loss,
all that time and all withdrawn,
wounds, defeats, a double-cross.

Lacking ears, I hear your wish.
Lacking eyes, I see your face.
Lacking touch, I touch your bliss.
Here we are in love's sweet grace.

Heal my heart, all it's made of.
Save my heart, repair the tie.
Strap my heart with wings of love.
Force my heart be made to fly.

Love,
Richelle

Letter to Humanity

Don't be a dick.
Don't be a pimp.
Don't be the rod of correction.
Don't be a cocks-man.
Don't take one for the team.
Don't grow a pair
Don't hold it in.
Don't command.
Don't man up.

Be a pussy.
Be a whore.
Be wet spaghetti.
Be a cunt.
Cry.
Be a pansy.
Show emotion.
Go queer on me.
Back down.
Be that sexy juice box.
Oh, is the little girl gonna cry?
Yes.

Love, Richelle

Letter to My Audience

Just so you understand,
I don't do trans,
to be chic.

I don't do trans,
to get off,
so to speak.

Your license,
I don't seek.

And I don't do trans,
to be your freak.

Love,
Richelle

On July 17, 1955, Richelle Lee Slota (formerly known as Richard) was one of 200 3rd Graders selected to open Disneyland by running across the draw bridge into Fantasyland. She's been running into Fantasyland ever since. She has published much poetry, *Famous Michael*, a chapbook, *Stray Son*, a novel, and, with co-author, Yaw Boateng, *Captive Market: Commercial Kidnapping Stories from Nigeria*, a non-fiction book. She earned a MA in Creative Writing from San Francisco State. She is a Meter Mentor to women learning meter on Annie Finch's online community, Poetry Witchery Community. She is an Army vet and has 3 adult children.